The Rescue of Winks

DIANE ODEGARD GOCKEL

DEDICATION

To my loving husband Don, who supports my love and work with
rescue animals and has encouraged me to write about them. And,
to all God's angels, like Winks, that have shared time on our farm.
I am so grateful to Him for this calling.

ABOUT THE AUTHOR

Diane Odegard Gockel is a former high school
teacher who has devoted much of her life to the
rescue, fostering and adoption of homeless pets.
She and her daughter Julie Diane Stafford co-
own Creative Kids Unplugged. Diane and her
husband Don have four grown children and live
on a small farm in Sammamish, Washington.

Other Books in the Rescue Series by
Diane Odegard Gockel

Bella Saves the Farm

Al the Alpaca: Forever Friends

Fancy Has a Plan

My name is Winks.

I got this name from the Farm Lady, whom I just call "the Lady." She nicknamed me Winks because I only have one eye and she loved how I always seem to be winking at her. To some, being a one-eyed cat could be a problem, but my problems used to be much bigger than that! Let me explain.

I lived in a house with a crazy cat lady and tons and tons of cats. No one petted us or paid much attention to our needs. I had an injury to my eye and it was never cared for, so I lost my sight in that eye. Then one day the people from the shelter came in and took most of us cats away. Six of the female cats were pregnant, and I was one of them. I was so scared. They put us in cages and brought us to the shelter to be adopted. The pregnant cats had to find foster homes first, until our babies were born, so it wasn't long before I was whisked off to an unfamiliar place.

When I got to my foster home, I was still very scared. I did not trust people because they had never seemed to be very kind to me. When my new foster parent opened my crate door, I quickly scampered out and crawled under the nearest bed to hide. My foster mom kept trying to grab me and pull me out from under the bed. It was then that I bit her. This caused my troubles to become even worse. Soon, the shelter people arrived wearing gloves, dragged me from my hiding spot, and brought me back to the shelter. I began to think I would live in a small metal cage for the rest of my life, which made me even more frightened.

It was that day when I saw the Farm Lady for the first time. She came into the shelter and chatted with the volunteers, whom she seemed to know. Her voice was calm and friendly. Finally, she looked at me and smiled, picked up my crate, and took me with her to my second foster home.

The Lady brought me to a room in her house and opened my crate door. Then I heard her quietly leave. I did not move, though. I waited until the room was silent and I knew I was alone. Only then did I peek out the crate window. I was in a huge room full of cat toys and a giant cat-climbing tree! *Is it a trick?* I wondered. I couldn't risk it. I played it safe and stayed in my crate all night.

By morning, my tummy was a rumbling, but I was too afraid to leave the safety of my crate. Soon, I heard footsteps and the door of the huge room opened. It was the Lady. Her kind voice greeted me, but she did not approach me. Instead, she walked across the room and busied herself with other tasks. All the while, she seemed to be talking to me. Her voice was soft, and her movements were slow and calming. Then she left.

That's when I smelled something wonderful! My tummy was so empty, and I could tell there was something tasty out there. I decided to plan my move carefully. I waited until I could not hear any footsteps or voices, and then I cautiously crawled out of my crate to follow the scent. I found the most delicious meal in a bowl right where the Lady had been working. *Did she leave that for me?* I wondered. I wasn't sure, but I ate the whole thing before heading back to my crate for a long catnap.

Days passed, and I began to see the huge room as not such a scary place. I spent more and more time outside my crate. The Lady left food twice a day and came in several times a day for visits. I always hissed at her when she reached out to pet me, but I didn't really mean to and the Lady never was afraid of my hissing. I was still untrusting and scared. I remember the day I finally let the Lady pet me. I didn't even move. She was gentle, so I began to trust her. At each visit, I would hiss at her, but then I would let her pet me. I would never let her pick me up. Never.

I knew the time was approaching for my kittens to be born. I needed to find somewhere private to have my babies. In the huge room, I discovered a box lined with towels and blankets. It was well hidden under the cat tree, and I knew it would be the perfect place. By morning, I shared the huge room with my three darling babies, whom the Lady named Chatter, Mouse, and Rascal. Chatter was a gray tabby and quite the talker; Mouse was all gray with a white spot under his neck; and Rascal, the little devil, looked just like me—all black.

Weeks went by, and as my kittens grew bigger and stronger, they began eating on their own. Nights were filled with Chatter talking away, Mouse hanging off the cat tree, and Rascal playing hide-and-seek with sudden surprise attacks from behind. My kittens loved the Lady! They would climb all over her, playing with her hair and shoelaces. And they would let her pick them up. All the cat toys were in full use, and life just couldn't have been any better.

But I feared that things would soon change. The Lady weighed my kittens every day, and once, I overheard her saying that they needed to weigh two pounds before we could return to the shelter and find permanent homes. As cute as my babies were, I knew they would get adopted to wonderful homes right away and be happy, but I wasn't so sure about my future.

See, kittens are usually the first to be adopted; everyone wants a cute little kitten. Friendly cats are next to find good homes. People like cats that sit on their laps and greet their guests. If you aren't a kitten and you aren't super friendly, then you had better be cute. People like the cute cats—fluffy, colorful, fancy cats. Kittens, friendly cats, and fancy cats all find homes. I was none of those things.

As you know, I wasn't friendly. Who would want a cat that hisses and doesn't like to be picked up? I certainly wasn't a kitten. And I was not a cute cat, either. I was a shorthaired black cat—the most common cat found at the shelter. I was also missing an eye. No, I was not a fancy cat. I feared for the day when I went back to the shelter and lived in a cage because no one wanted me. This made me even more afraid.

Finally, the day came to leave the huge room. The Lady filled the crate with my kittens and me, and we were off to the shelter. I knew that Rascal, Mouse, and Chatter were ready to find new homes of their own, and I was not worried for them. I had my own worries.

When we got to the shelter, the Lady said her good-byes to the kittens, but before I could say good-bye, I was whisked off to surgery to have my eye socket sewn up. I never got to say good-bye to the Lady. I wanted to thank her for giving me a safe place to live and for making me a better cat. I would never forget her, and I would miss her terribly.

The next thing I remember was feeling groggy after waking up from my surgery. I hoped my eye would look a little more attractive, because I knew the adoptions room would be my next stop. My eye was sore, and I was tired, and I just wanted to go home. But I didn't have a home. I began to panic. Who would want me? How long would I be in the shelter before I found a home of my own? Was there anyone out there who would give a one-eyed, unfriendly adult cat a home and a chance to be his or her devoted companion?

Just as I was feeling more alert, a shelter worker put me back in a crate and took me to another room—which I assumed was adoptions. I did not recognize this room at all, however, and I had never felt more alone. Just when I was about to meow for help, I heard the rattling of my crate door as someone opened it. I could hardly believe my eyes! It was the Lady! I didn't hiss this time. I was so glad to see her! She reached in my crate and picked me up for the first time. Then she gave me a little kiss and said, "C'mon, Winks, let's go home!"

The real Winks

Winks' real Kittens; Chatter, Mouse and Rascal